PRINCEWILL LAGANG

Intergenerational Relationships: Bridging the Gap

First published by PRINCEWILL LAGANG 2023

Copyright © 2023 by Princewill Lagang

All rights reserved. No part of this publication may be reproduced, stored or transmitted in any form or by any means, electronic, mechanical, photocopying, recording, scanning, or otherwise without written permission from the publisher. It is illegal to copy this book, post it to a website, or distribute it by any other means without permission.

Princewill Lagang asserts the moral right to be identified as the author of this work.

First edition

This book was professionally typeset on Reedsy.
Find out more at reedsy.com

Contents

1	Introduction	1
2	The Dynamics of Intergenerational Relationships	4
3	Cultural and Historical Context	7
4	Communication Styles Across Generations	10
5	Navigating Generational Differences	13
6	Technology and Digital Divide in Intergenerational...	16
7	Passing Down Wisdom and Knowledge	19
8	Supporting Each Other's Goals	22
9	Nurturing Family Bonds	25
10	Caring for Elderly Relatives	28
11	Learning from Each Other	31
12	Preserving Memories and Legacy	34

1

Introduction

In today's rapidly evolving world, where technology, culture, and values are constantly shifting, the intricate tapestry of relationships between different generations has taken on new complexity. This book sets out on a journey to delve into these relationships, aiming to illuminate the dynamics, challenges, and rewards that arise when individuals from diverse age groups come together.

The Significance of Inter-Generational Understanding:

At the heart of this exploration lies a fundamental truth: the connections we forge across generations are paramount to the sustenance of societal harmony, growth, and progress. As societies become more diverse, both in terms of age and culture, the need to understand and foster inter-generational connections becomes increasingly essential.

Understanding the diverse perspectives, values, and life experiences of different generations is vital for fostering empathy, empathy that can bridge gaps in communication and help resolve conflicts. When we appreciate the context in which each generation grew up, the historical events that shaped their worldviews, and the unique challenges they faced, we gain a deeper insight into their motivations and aspirations. This understanding forms the bedrock upon which we can build relationships that transcend age barriers.

Exploring the Dynamics:

Throughout this book, we will embark on a comprehensive exploration of the dynamics that exist between generations. From the Baby Boomers who witnessed significant societal transformations, to the Gen Xers who navigated the advent of technology, to the Millennials and Gen Z who have grown up in a digital age, each generation has distinct perspectives, communication styles, and values.

These dynamics manifest not only in family settings but also in workplaces, communities, and even in broader global discussions. Recognizing the strengths and weaknesses of different age groups allows us to harness their collective potential, generating innovative solutions to complex problems and capitalizing on the wisdom of experience.

The Structure of the Book:

As we proceed through the chapters, we will delve into specific aspects of inter-generational relationships. We will explore how generational differences influence communication patterns, decision-making processes, and even leisure activities. We will discuss the challenges that can arise due to misunderstandings and biases, while also presenting strategies to overcome these hurdles and build bridges between generations.

Furthermore, we will examine the role of education and mentorship in facilitating inter-generational understanding. By fostering an environment of reciprocal learning, we can ensure that knowledge and experiences are passed down while embracing the fresh perspectives and innovative ideas of younger generations.

INTRODUCTION

Conclusion:

In a world where the pace of change seems to accelerate with each passing day, the exploration of inter-generational relationships takes on profound importance. By embracing the diversity of experiences and perspectives that different age groups bring to the table, we can forge connections that enrich our lives, enhance our communities, and propel society forward into a future that is united in purpose and understanding. This book is an invitation to embark on this exploration, to learn, to empathize, and to build bridges that span the generations.

2

The Dynamics of Intergenerational Relationships

Intergenerational relationships are the threads that weave the fabric of society, connecting individuals of different ages through shared experiences, values, and aspirations. This chapter delves into the intricate nature of these relationships, exploring the dynamics that underlie them and the significance they hold in fostering social cohesion and personal growth.

The Complexity of Intergenerational Relationships:

At the heart of intergenerational dynamics lies a complexity born of divergent life experiences, cultural contexts, and historical events. Each generation has been shaped by its own unique set of circumstances, leading to distinct perspectives and ways of interacting with the world. This complexity can either serve as a source of enrichment or a barrier to understanding, depending on how it is approached.

Challenges of Bridging the Generation Gap:

Bridging the generation gap is not without its challenges. Communication can be hindered by differences in communication styles and the use of technology. Misunderstandings may arise due to varying attitudes toward work, family, and societal norms. Additionally, stereotypes and biases can perpetuate misunderstandings and contribute to conflict between generations.

Benefits of Bridging the Generation Gap:

However, the rewards of bridging the generation gap are substantial. By embracing the differences that exist between generations, we gain access to a wealth of knowledge, wisdom, and diverse perspectives. Older generations can share their experiences, offering insights into history, resilience, and life lessons. Meanwhile, younger generations bring fresh perspectives, innovative ideas, and a keen awareness of evolving societal trends.

The interplay of these perspectives creates a synergy that can lead to transformative change. Innovation often arises at the intersection of different generations, where traditional wisdom combines with contemporary knowledge to generate creative solutions to modern challenges.

Fostering Personal Growth and Societal Cohesion:

Intergenerational relationships contribute not only to personal growth but also to societal cohesion. Through these relationships, individuals develop empathy, tolerance, and an understanding of diverse viewpoints. This understanding forms the basis for constructive dialogue, conflict resolution, and collaborative efforts that transcend generational lines.

Furthermore, intergenerational relationships can act as a safeguard against isolation and ageism. When individuals of different ages interact and form meaningful connections, stereotypes and biases are challenged, leading to a more inclusive and supportive community.

Conclusion:

The dynamics of intergenerational relationships are a testament to the rich tapestry of human experiences. While challenges may arise due to differences in perspectives and life experiences, the benefits of bridging the generation gap far outweigh the difficulties. As we navigate this dynamic landscape, we have the opportunity to learn from one another, enrich our lives, and contribute to a more harmonious and united society. This chapter invites us to explore the intricacies of these relationships, embracing the potential for growth and connection that lies within them.

3

Cultural and Historical Context

Cultural and historical factors are potent forces that shape the contours of intergenerational dynamics, infusing relationships with depth, meaning, and complexity. This chapter delves into the profound impact of cultural heritage and historical events on intergenerational relationships, examining how values, beliefs, and experiences from the past continue to reverberate in the present.

Cultural Heritage as a Lens:

Cultural heritage serves as a lens through which each generation views the world. From traditions and rituals to language and social norms, these cultural elements provide a framework for understanding and navigating life. They also influence how individuals relate to others, including those from different generations.

The interplay of cultural heritage across generations can lead to both harmonious interactions and occasional friction. Differences in values, communication styles, and expectations can emerge due to varying degrees of adherence to cultural norms. However, these differences also present an opportunity for mutual learning and growth, as individuals exchange insights and experiences that reflect their distinct cultural backgrounds.

Historical Events as Shared Experiences:

Historical events play a crucial role in shaping the perspectives and attitudes of different generations. Whether it's a world-changing event like a war, a technological revolution, or a social movement, these experiences leave an indelible mark on the collective consciousness. They influence how each generation perceives the world, responds to challenges, and envisions the future.

The echoes of historical events can be both unifying and divisive. Shared experiences can foster a sense of solidarity, with older generations imparting lessons learned from past struggles and achievements. On the other hand, generational conflicts might arise when differing interpretations of historical events clash, leading to debates over values, justice, and societal progress.

Values, Beliefs, and Perspectives:

Values and beliefs are the building blocks of intergenerational relationships. Each generation carries its own set of values and beliefs, often shaped by the cultural and historical context in which they grew up. These values influence decisions, priorities, and behaviors, and they contribute to the ways in which individuals relate to one another.

Understanding and appreciating these values is essential for bridging generational gaps. The beliefs held by older generations might underscore the importance of tradition, stability, and continuity. Younger generations, meanwhile, might emphasize adaptability, innovation, and social change. By acknowledging the legitimacy of these different perspectives, intergenerational relationships can become enriched by mutual respect and a shared sense of purpose.

Conclusion:

Cultural heritage and historical context are powerful forces that infuse intergenerational relationships with depth and significance. By recognizing the influence of these factors, we gain insights into the diverse perspectives and motivations that each generation brings to the table. Through this understanding, we can navigate the complexities of intergenerational dynamics with empathy, respect, and a commitment to fostering connections that transcend time and experience. This chapter invites us to appreciate the intricate interplay between culture, history, and relationships, encouraging us to embrace the tapestry of human experience that binds generations together.

4

Communication Styles Across Generations

Communication serves as the cornerstone of intergenerational relationships, enabling the exchange of ideas, emotions, and experiences. However, the distinct communication styles of different age groups can sometimes lead to misunderstandings and barriers. This chapter delves into the variations in communication styles among generations and offers strategies for adapting communication to foster effective understanding and connection.

The Evolution of Communication:

Generational differences in communication styles are often rooted in the technological and cultural shifts that have occurred over time. Older generations may place a greater emphasis on face-to-face communication, valuing direct interactions and traditional forms of expression. In contrast, younger generations, who have grown up in the digital age, might be more comfortable with rapid, text-based communication and the use of visual media.

Understanding these differences is essential to transcending communication barriers. By recognizing that various generations have distinct preferences and comfort levels with different communication platforms, we can establish a foundation for meaningful dialogue.

Adapting Communication for Understanding:

Adapting communication styles across generations involves a delicate balance of respecting tradition while embracing innovation. Here are some strategies to enhance effective understanding:

1. Active Listening: Actively listen to what individuals from different generations are saying. Pay attention to their choice of words, tone, and nonverbal cues. This demonstrates respect and attentiveness, which can help bridge gaps in communication.

2. Flexibility: Recognize that there is no one-size-fits-all approach to communication. Be willing to adjust your communication style based on the preferences and comfort levels of those you are interacting with.

3. Clarity and Context: When discussing complex topics, provide clear explanations and context. Older generations might require more detailed information, while younger generations might appreciate succinct summaries.

4. Empathy: Put yourself in the shoes of the person you are communicating with. Consider their background, experiences, and perspective to tailor your communication approach accordingly.

5. Use of Technology: If engaging with younger generations, be open to using technology for communication, such as texting, social media, or video calls. Likewise, when communicating with older generations, prioritize face-to-face conversations or phone calls if possible.

6. Storytelling: Share stories and experiences from your own generation to create a bridge of understanding. This can help younger generations appreciate the context in which older individuals have lived.

7. Patience: Recognize that generational differences can lead to misunderstandings. Be patient and willing to explain, clarify, and engage in open dialogue to resolve any misconceptions.

Conclusion:

Effective communication is the linchpin that holds intergenerational relationships together. By acknowledging and adapting to differences in communication styles, we can break down barriers and foster meaningful connections. This chapter encourages us to approach communication with empathy, flexibility, and an openness to learning from one another. By bridging the gap in communication, we can cultivate relationships that thrive on mutual respect, understanding, and the power of shared experiences across generations.

5

Navigating Generational Differences

Generational differences in attitudes, values, and preferences are natural products of evolving societal norms and experiences. However, these differences can sometimes lead to challenges in understanding and communication. This chapter delves into common generational disparities and provides strategies for fostering respectful dialogue and finding common ground among diverse age groups.

Identifying Generational Differences:

Generational differences can encompass a wide range of aspects, including work ethic, communication styles, technology usage, social values, and perspectives on family and societal roles. For instance, while older generations might prioritize job stability and traditional family structures, younger generations might value flexibility, work-life balance, and inclusivity.

Acknowledging these differences is essential for fostering mutual understanding. By recognizing that each generation's perspectives are influenced by their unique historical and cultural contexts, we can approach conversations with a spirit of empathy and respect.

Strategies for Respectful Dialogue:

1. Active Listening: Engage in active listening to understand the viewpoints of individuals from different generations. This involves giving them your full attention, asking open-ended questions, and refraining from making assumptions.

2. Avoid Stereotyping: Generational stereotypes can perpetuate misunderstandings. Instead of assuming that a particular trait applies to an entire generation, approach each person as an individual with their own unique experiences and perspectives.

3. Ask Questions: Pose questions that encourage dialogue and reflection. Asking about experiences, challenges, and values can create opportunities for meaningful conversations that bridge generational gaps.

4. Empathetic Language: Use language that demonstrates empathy and respect. Phrases like "I understand where you're coming from" or "Tell me more about your perspective" signal your willingness to engage without judgment.

5. Share Personal Experiences: Openly share your own experiences and values to provide context for your viewpoints. This can help others understand the factors that have shaped your perspective.

Finding Common Ground:

1. Shared Goals: Identify common goals that transcend generational differences. Whether it's creating a harmonious family environment or achieving workplace success, finding shared objectives can unite individuals from diverse age groups.

2. Focus on Values: Explore the underlying values that drive each generation's

beliefs and behaviors. By understanding the motivations behind differing viewpoints, you can identify areas of alignment.

3. Learning Exchange: Embrace the concept of a learning exchange, where both older and younger generations can impart their knowledge and experiences to one another. This promotes a sense of reciprocity and mutual growth.

4. Collaborative Problem Solving: Address challenges collaboratively by seeking solutions that incorporate insights from different generations. This not only leads to more creative solutions but also reinforces the idea that diverse perspectives are assets.

Conclusion:

Generational differences offer an opportunity for growth, learning, and the expansion of our perspectives. This chapter encourages us to approach these differences with a spirit of curiosity and openness. By engaging in respectful dialogue, actively listening, and seeking common ground, we can transcend generational divides and build relationships that are characterized by understanding, cooperation, and a shared commitment to collective well-being. As we navigate the complexities of generational differences, we pave the way for a more harmonious and connected society that benefits from the wisdom and innovation of every age group.

6

Technology and Digital Divide in Intergenerational Relationships

Technology has revolutionized the way we live, work, and connect with one another. However, its influence is not uniform across generations, leading to what is known as the "digital divide." This chapter explores the impact of technology on intergenerational relationships and provides strategies for bridging this divide to foster meaningful connections.

The Digital Divide and Its Implications:

The digital divide refers to the gap in access to and use of technology between different generations. Younger generations, such as Millennials and Gen Z, have grown up with technology as an integral part of their lives, while older generations might face challenges in adapting to digital tools and platforms. This divide can lead to miscommunications, isolation, and feelings of exclusion among those who are less tech-savvy.

Understanding the Impact:

Technology can both unite and divide generations. On one hand, it offers platforms for sharing experiences, staying connected, and engaging in collective discussions. On the other hand, overreliance on digital communication can hinder face-to-face interactions and erode the depth of personal connections.

Bridging the Digital Divide:

1. Education and Training: Provide opportunities for older generations to learn about technology through workshops, classes, or one-on-one tutorials. This empowers them to use digital tools for communication, information access, and entertainment.

2. Patience and Support: Younger generations can offer patient support and guidance to older family members or colleagues who are less familiar with technology. Approach teaching with empathy and understanding.

3. Multigenerational Collaboration: Collaborate on technology-related projects that involve members from different age groups. This could range from creating a family website to collectively curating digital photo albums.

4. Shared Experiences: Use technology as a means to create shared experiences. This could involve participating in virtual events, online games, or video calls that bring generations together despite physical distance.

5. Balance: Encourage a balance between digital and in-person interactions. While technology facilitates connections, it's important to maintain the richness of face-to-face conversations and shared activities.

6. Open Dialogue: Have open discussions about the benefits and drawbacks of technology in intergenerational relationships. Address concerns, share perspectives, and collectively establish guidelines for respectful and meaningful online interactions.

Conclusion:

Technology is a powerful tool that can strengthen intergenerational relationships by transcending geographical barriers and enabling connections. However, its benefits are most potent when the digital divide is addressed. This chapter emphasizes the importance of embracing technology as a means to enhance communication and foster connections, while also recognizing the value of in-person interactions and traditional forms of communication. By bridging the digital divide, we can create a harmonious blend of modernity and tradition, allowing generations to learn from and support one another in a rapidly changing world.

7

Passing Down Wisdom and Knowledge

One of the most profound ways in which intergenerational relationships enrich our lives is through the transmission of wisdom and knowledge from one generation to the next. This chapter delves into the significance of passing down experiences and insights, highlighting the mutual benefits of such exchanges, and offering strategies to create platforms for sharing stories.

The Importance of Passing Down Wisdom:

Throughout history, societies have recognized the value of passing down wisdom as a means of preserving cultural heritage, life lessons, and accumulated knowledge. The experiences of older generations provide a treasure trove of insights that can guide younger generations in navigating life's challenges, making informed decisions, and finding meaning in their journey.

The reciprocal nature of passing down wisdom is striking. While older generations share their stories and experiences, they also gain a renewed sense of purpose and connection. Younger generations, in turn, gain access to valuable lessons that help them contextualize their own experiences within the broader tapestry of human existence.

Creating Platforms for Sharing Stories:

1. Family Gatherings: Family events and gatherings provide an ideal setting for intergenerational story sharing. Designate a time for storytelling sessions where family members of all ages can recount their experiences and anecdotes.

2. Oral Tradition: Embrace the age-old tradition of oral storytelling. Encourage older family members to share stories from their past, whether they are personal anecdotes, historical events, or cultural narratives.

3. Digital Archives: Create digital platforms, such as family websites or social media groups, where stories, photos, and videos can be shared and preserved for future generations to access and enjoy.

4. Personal Journals: Encourage older individuals to maintain personal journals or memoirs that chronicle their life experiences, values, and reflections. These written accounts can be shared with family members or kept as a cherished family heirloom.

5. Mentorship Programs: Extend the practice of passing down wisdom beyond the family unit. Establish mentorship programs in schools, workplaces, or communities to facilitate meaningful connections and knowledge exchange between generations.

6. Storytelling Workshops: Organize workshops that provide a structured environment for intergenerational storytelling. These workshops can help individuals refine their storytelling skills while facilitating an exchange of experiences.

Conclusion:

PASSING DOWN WISDOM AND KNOWLEDGE

Passing down wisdom and knowledge is a sacred tradition that bridges generations and perpetuates the tapestry of human experience. This chapter celebrates the value of sharing stories and insights as a means of fostering deeper connections, preserving cultural heritage, and facilitating personal growth. By creating platforms for intergenerational storytelling, we create a space where the lessons of the past become guiding lights for the future. Through the act of sharing and listening, we honor the wisdom of those who came before us and create a legacy of understanding, empathy, and shared humanity.

8

Supporting Each Other's Goals

Intergenerational relationships offer a unique opportunity to provide support and encouragement in the pursuit of individual and collective aspirations. This chapter delves into the vital role of support in nurturing one another's dreams, highlighting the benefits of such collaboration, and offering strategies for fostering an environment where each generation's goals are valued and uplifted.

The Role of Support in Aspirations:

Support is the cornerstone of intergenerational relationships that empower individuals to chase their dreams. When generations come together to offer guidance, resources, and emotional backing, it not only propels individual success but also strengthens the bonds that connect different age groups.

By supporting each other's goals, individuals across generations contribute to a collective sense of purpose and shared achievement. This creates a dynamic in which each person's accomplishments become a source of pride and inspiration for the entire family or community.

Encouraging Each Other's Dreams:

1. Active Listening: Pay attention to the aspirations and goals of individuals from different generations. Ask questions to understand their passions and motivations, and express genuine interest in their pursuits.

2. Validation: Validate the dreams and aspirations of others by acknowledging their significance and worth. This acknowledgment fosters a sense of empowerment and confidence.

3. Collaborative Approach: Identify opportunities for collaboration between generations. Pool resources, skills, and insights to jointly work towards common goals or to support each other's individual endeavors.

4. Mentorship: Older generations can serve as mentors, offering guidance based on their experiences. Younger generations, in turn, can provide fresh perspectives and innovative ideas that contribute to the pursuit of shared goals.

5. Open Communication: Create an open dialogue where family members can openly share their goals, fears, and challenges. This environment encourages mutual understanding and empathy.

6. Celebrate Achievements: Recognize and celebrate the achievements of individuals from all age groups. This can be as simple as a heartfelt congratulation or as elaborate as a family gathering to commemorate milestones.

7. Provide Resources: When possible, offer practical support such as financial assistance, time, or skills to help individuals reach their goals. This demonstrates a commitment to each other's success.

Conclusion:

Supporting each other's goals is a powerful way to cultivate intergenerational relationships that thrive on mutual growth and encouragement. By embracing the dreams and aspirations of individuals from different generations, we create a nurturing environment that fuels personal achievement while also strengthening the bonds that connect us. This chapter encourages us to actively engage in uplifting one another, recognizing that the success of one generation contributes to the collective prosperity of all. Through the act of support, we build a legacy of unity, collaboration, and the unwavering belief in each other's potential.

9

Nurturing Family Bonds

Strong family bonds are a cornerstone of intergenerational relationships, providing a sense of belonging, support, and continuity across generations. This chapter delves into the profound significance of maintaining these bonds and offers insights into the role of family traditions and gatherings in fostering connection and unity.

The Significance of Family Bonds:

Family bonds form the foundation upon which individuals develop a sense of identity, values, and emotional security. These bonds provide a safety net in times of need, a source of celebration during milestones, and a shared history that connects generations across time.

In a rapidly changing world, family bonds offer a sense of constancy and stability. They serve as a reminder of where one comes from and instill a sense of purpose rooted in a larger collective identity. Moreover, strong family ties are associated with improved mental health, greater resilience, and enhanced overall well-being.

Family Traditions and Their Role:

Family traditions act as threads that weave generations together. These rituals and customs, whether simple or elaborate, create a sense of continuity and belonging. They offer an opportunity to pass down cultural heritage, values, and stories that enrich the fabric of family life.

Traditions provide a sense of rhythm and predictability, anchoring family members in shared experiences and memories. Whether it's celebrating holidays, participating in annual events, or engaging in specific practices, these traditions create touchpoints that connect different generations despite changing circumstances.

The Importance of Family Gatherings:

Family gatherings are occasions where the tapestry of family bonds is woven even tighter. These events offer a space for intergenerational interaction, shared laughter, and meaningful conversations. They provide a chance for older generations to share their wisdom and experiences, while younger generations infuse the family with youthful energy and innovation.

Family gatherings also play a crucial role in building memories that endure for a lifetime. The stories shared, the experiences enjoyed, and the connections forged during these gatherings become cherished legacies that are carried forward by successive generations.

Nurturing Family Bonds:

1. Regular Communication: Maintain open lines of communication among family members through phone calls, video chats, or messaging apps. Share updates, stories, and moments of daily life to create a sense of connection.

2. Document Family History: Encourage older generations to share their

stories and memories. Documenting family history through written accounts, photos, or oral recordings ensures that these narratives are preserved for future generations.

3. Create New Traditions: Develop new traditions that reflect the values and interests of different generations. This can include activities that bring family members together regularly, fostering a sense of continuity.

4. Plan Family Gatherings: Organize family gatherings that provide opportunities for bonding and sharing experiences. These gatherings can be formal or informal, large or intimate, but they should prioritize connection.

5. Celebrate Milestones: Celebrate milestones, achievements, and birthdays as a family. These occasions create opportunities to express love, appreciation, and encouragement.

Conclusion:

Nurturing family bonds is a labor of love that reaps lifelong rewards. Family traditions and gatherings are the cornerstones of intergenerational connections, offering a sense of belonging and shared history. This chapter underscores the importance of investing time and effort into cultivating family bonds, recognizing that these relationships provide a source of strength, support, and joy that enriches the lives of all family members. Through the preservation of traditions and the celebration of togetherness, we honor the legacy of those who came before us and lay the groundwork for a future that is united in love and shared memories.

10

Caring for Elderly Relatives

Caring for elderly relatives is a significant aspect of intergenerational relationships, where roles may reverse as younger generations become caregivers to their elders. This chapter delves into the responsibilities, challenges, and rewards of caring for elderly family members. It also offers strategies to provide support while maintaining the dignity and well-being of those receiving care.

The Responsibilities and Challenges of Caregiving:

Caring for elderly relatives involves a range of responsibilities, from assisting with daily activities to managing healthcare needs. As parents and grandparents age, they might require help with tasks that were once routine, such as cooking, cleaning, and personal care. Additionally, medical conditions and cognitive changes might necessitate more intensive care, including medication management and emotional support.

Caregiving can be emotionally demanding and physically exhausting. Balancing caregiving with personal and professional responsibilities can lead to stress, burnout, and a sense of isolation. It's important to recognize that caregiving is a journey that requires careful planning and self-care.

Providing Support and Maintaining Dignity:

1. Open Communication: Initiate honest conversations about your elderly relative's needs, preferences, and wishes. Collaborate to develop a care plan that respects their autonomy while addressing their requirements.

2. Respect Dignity: Prioritize your loved one's dignity by involving them in decision-making and respecting their choices. Ensure that they are comfortable and empowered throughout the caregiving process.

3. Seek Professional Help: Consult medical professionals and seek advice from experts in elderly care. This ensures that your loved one's physical and emotional well-being is properly addressed.

4. Create a Support System: Enlist the help of other family members, friends, and support groups. Sharing caregiving responsibilities can lighten the load and provide opportunities for social interaction.

5. Embrace Self-Care: Caregiving is physically and emotionally demanding, so prioritize your own well-being. Make time for activities you enjoy, seek respite care, and don't hesitate to ask for help when needed.

6. Modify the Home Environment: Create a safe and accessible living space for your elderly relative. This might involve making modifications to accommodate mobility challenges or cognitive impairments.

7. Engage in Meaningful Activities: Foster a sense of purpose and engagement for your loved one through activities they enjoy, such as hobbies, music, art, or spending time with family and friends.

8. Regular Health Checkups: Ensure that your elderly relative receives regular

health checkups and screenings. Address any medical concerns promptly to maintain their well-being.

Conclusion:

Caring for elderly relatives is an expression of love, respect, and compassion that nurtures intergenerational bonds. While it presents challenges, caregiving is an opportunity to give back to those who have nurtured us throughout our lives. This chapter emphasizes the importance of providing support in a way that respects the dignity and autonomy of elderly family members. By engaging in open communication, seeking professional guidance, and practicing self-care, caregivers can navigate the complexities of caregiving while creating an environment that promotes the well-being of all family members involved. Through this journey, intergenerational relationships evolve into a beautiful tapestry woven with love, empathy, and shared experiences.

11

Learning from Each Other

Intergenerational relationships offer a unique platform for mutual learning, where individuals from different age groups share their experiences, perspectives, and knowledge. This chapter delves into the enriching process of learning from one another, highlighting how diverse generations can draw wisdom, insight, and inspiration from each other's life journeys.

The Power of Mutual Learning:

Intergenerational relationships present a rich opportunity for cross-generational learning that transcends traditional education. Each generation brings a unique set of experiences, skills, and viewpoints that contribute to a holistic understanding of the world. By engaging in open dialogue, individuals can gain insights into different historical contexts, cultural shifts, and personal narratives.

This exchange of knowledge creates a dynamic in which both younger and older generations are learners and teachers, enriching one another's lives with new perspectives and a deeper appreciation for the diverse tapestry of human experiences.

Learning from Different Life Stages:

1. Experience and Wisdom: Older generations possess a wealth of life experience and wisdom accumulated over the years. Younger generations can learn from these stories and insights, gaining a broader perspective on challenges, choices, and personal growth.

2. Adaptability and Innovation: Younger generations bring a fresh perspective and innovative ideas shaped by contemporary circumstances. Older generations can learn from their adaptability and the creative solutions they bring to modern challenges.

3. Values and Traditions: Sharing cultural values and traditions is a powerful way to bridge generations. Younger individuals can learn about their heritage, while older individuals can understand the evolving priorities and concerns of younger generations.

4. Technological Literacy: Younger generations are often more adept with technology. Older individuals can learn from their younger counterparts, acquiring new skills that allow them to navigate the digital age more confidently.

5. Resilience and Growth: Learning from the resilience and coping strategies of older generations can provide younger individuals with valuable tools to navigate life's difficulties and uncertainties.

Strategies for Facilitating Mutual Learning:

1. Active Listening: Listen attentively to the stories and experiences shared by individuals from different generations. Ask questions that encourage them to elaborate on their journeys and perspectives.

2. Share Stories: Create an environment where individuals feel comfortable sharing their stories and insights. This can be done through formal storytelling sessions or casual conversations.

3. Celebrate Diversity: Embrace the diversity of perspectives and experiences that different generations bring to the table. Avoid judgment and foster an environment of respect and curiosity.

4. Formal Learning Exchanges: Organize structured learning exchanges where individuals from different generations can teach each other specific skills, such as cooking, gardening, or crafts.

5. Intergenerational Projects: Collaborate on projects that require the skills and knowledge of individuals from different age groups. This could include family history research, community service, or creative endeavors.

Conclusion:

Mutual learning is a cornerstone of intergenerational relationships, where the exchange of experiences and insights creates a dynamic of growth and understanding. By embracing the diverse perspectives that different generations offer, we enrich our lives, broaden our horizons, and foster a sense of unity that transcends time. This chapter underscores the profound value of learning from each other and encourages us to approach intergenerational interactions with openness, respect, and a genuine desire to absorb the wisdom that each generation brings. Through this process, we contribute to a legacy of shared knowledge and continuous growth that binds generations together in a tapestry of shared understanding.

12

Preserving Memories and Legacy

Intergenerational connections are the threads that weave together the fabric of our personal and collective legacies. This final chapter reflects on the profound impact of these relationships on the preservation of memories and the creation of a lasting legacy. It summarizes key takeaways from the book and offers guidance for building enduring and meaningful relationships across generations.

The Impact on Legacy:

Intergenerational relationships play a pivotal role in shaping our legacies. Through these connections, memories, values, and stories are passed down from one generation to the next, creating a bridge that spans time and enriches our understanding of the past. These connections allow us to see ourselves as part of a continuum, where our actions today influence the trajectory of future generations.

Legacy is not just about material wealth; it encompasses the lessons, experiences, and relationships we leave behind. Intergenerational connections breathe life into this legacy by carrying forward the essence of who we are and what we stand for.

Key Takeaways:

1. Diverse Perspectives: Intergenerational relationships provide a platform for diverse perspectives and experiences to coexist. These differences enrich our understanding of the world and foster personal growth.

2. Communication: Effective communication is the cornerstone of successful intergenerational relationships. Active listening, empathy, and respectful dialogue create connections that transcend generational gaps.

3. Learning: Each generation has something valuable to teach and learn from the other. Mutual learning fosters growth, understanding, and a sense of unity that bridges generations.

4. Support and Care: Caring for elderly family members is a testament to the strength of intergenerational bonds. Providing support while respecting dignity creates an environment of love and compassion.

5. Traditions and Stories: Family traditions and stories serve as the glue that binds generations together. These shared experiences create touchpoints that connect family members across time.

6. Legacy Building: Intergenerational connections are the foundation of legacy building. By passing down values, wisdom, and memories, we contribute to a legacy that extends beyond our individual lifetimes.

Guidance for Building Lasting Relationships:

1. Prioritize Connection: Make an effort to prioritize time for interactions with individuals from different generations. Meaningful connections don't happen by chance; they require deliberate effort.

2. Embrace Openness: Approach intergenerational relationships with an open heart and mind. Be curious, ask questions, and be willing to learn from one another.

3. Respect Differences: Differences in values, perspectives, and life experiences are natural. Approach these differences with respect and a willingness to understand.

4. Celebrate Milestones: Recognize and celebrate milestones, both big and small. These occasions provide opportunities to come together as a family and create cherished memories.

5. Share Stories: Encourage the sharing of stories and experiences. These narratives create a sense of continuity and provide insight into the lives of previous generations.

6. Practice Empathy: Put yourself in the shoes of individuals from different generations. Consider their perspectives, challenges, and joys to foster understanding and empathy.

Conclusion:

Intergenerational connections are the lifelines that connect us to our past, illuminate our present, and shape the trajectory of our future. By nurturing these relationships, we contribute to a legacy that transcends time and enriches the lives of generations to come. This final chapter reflects on the impact of intergenerational connections on preserving memories and creating a lasting legacy. It invites us to continue building these relationships with intention, empathy, and a deep appreciation for the transformative power of shared experiences and shared love across the ages.